21st Century
Basic Skills
Library

YOUR HEALTHY PLATE
DAIRY

by Katie Marsico

Cherry Lake Publishing • Ann Arbor, Michigan

3

Published in the United States of America
by Cherry Lake Publishing
Ann Arbor, Michigan
www.cherrylakepublishing.com

Content Adviser: Theresa A. Wilson, MS, RD, LD, Baylor College of Medicine, USDA/ARS Children's Nutrition Research Center, Houston, Texas

Photo Credits: Cover and page 1, ©Morgan Lane Photography/Shutterstock, Inc.; page 4, ©Larisa Lofitskaya/Shutterstock, Inc.; page 6, ©Richard Williamson/Shutterstock, Inc.; page 8, U.S. Department of Agriculture; page 10, ©MANDY GODBEHEAR/Shutterstock, Inc.; page 12, ©Blend Images/Alamy; page 14, ©Thomas Imo/Alamy; page 16, ©Jacek Chabraszewski/Dreamstime.com; page 18, ©Enigma/Alamy; page 20, ©wavebreakmedia ltd/Shutterstock, Inc.

Library of Congress Cataloging-in-Publication Data
Marsico, Katie, 1980–
  Your healthy plate. Dairy / by Katie Marsico.
    p. cm.—(21st century basic skills library. Level 3)
  Includes bibliographical references and index.
  ISBN 978-1-61080-350-2 (lib. bdg.)—ISBN 978-1-61080-357-1 (e-book)—ISBN 978-1-61080-398-4 (pbk.)
1. Dairy products—Juvenile literature. 2. Dairy products in human nutrition—Juvenile literature. I. Title. II. Title: Dairy.
  TX377.M368 2012
  641.6'7—dc23   2011034535

Cherry Lake Publishing would like to acknowledge the work of The Partnership for 21st Century Skills.
Please visit *www.21stcenturyskills.org* for more information.

Printed in the United States of America
Corporate Graphics Inc.
January 2012
CLSP10

TABLE OF CONTENTS

What Is Dairy?

Do you drink milk? Do you like eating yogurt and cheese?

These are **dairy** foods. They are made from milk.

Dairy **products** often come from the milk of cows.

Some farmers also **raise** goats or sheep for their milk.

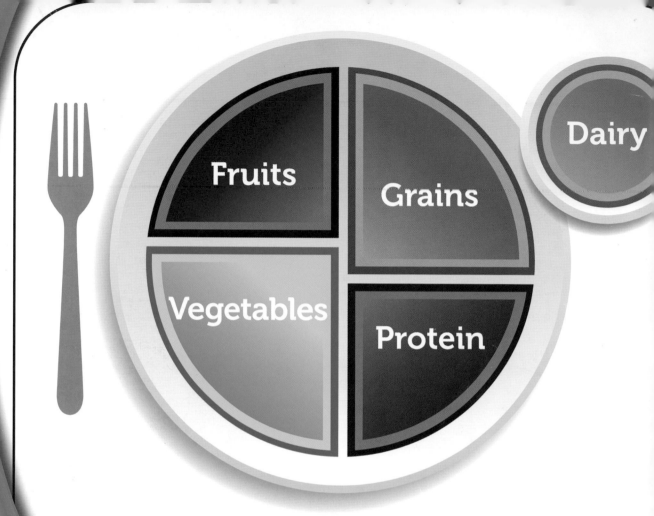

ChooseMyPlate.gov

Why Do You Need Dairy?

There are five main **food groups**. Dairy is one of the groups.

You should eat foods from all five groups. That will give you a **balanced diet**.

Why should you eat dairy products?

Dairy foods help your bones grow. They also help your muscles grow strong.

How can you make dairy part of your diet?

First, you need to know how much dairy to eat.

Kids your age should have two to three **servings** of dairy each day.

Think of foods that could make up your daily servings.

What Dairy Foods Should You Eat?

Drinking milk is a good way to add dairy to your diet.

So is eating a cup of yogurt. You can also eat two slices of cheese.

Eat dairy foods that are low in **fat**. Low-fat dairy foods are better for your heart.

They are also good for other parts of your body.

Do you need help choosing low-fat dairy foods?

Ask an adult to help you find healthy dairy products!

Find Out More

BOOK

Dilkes, D. H. *Milk and Dairy*. Berkeley Heights, NJ: Enslow Elementary, 2012.

WEB SITE

United States Department of Agriculture (USDA)—Food Groups: Dairy
www.choosemyplate.gov/foodgroups/dairy.html
Learn more about dairy foods and how to make them part of your diet.

Glossary

balanced diet (BAL-uhntzd DYE-it) eating just the right amounts of different foods

dairy (DARE-ee) foods that are made from milk or that have milk in them

fat (FAT) oil found in certain kinds of foods

food groups (FOOD GROOPS) groups of different foods that people should have in their diets

products (PRAH-duhkts) items that are made to be sold

raise (RAYZ) to take care of an animal until it is grown

servings (SURV-ingz) set amounts of food

Home and School Connection

Use this list of words from the book to help your child become a better reader. Word games and writing activities can help beginning readers reinforce literacy skills.

a	could	five	kids	other	think
add	cows	food	know	part	three
adult	cup	foods	like	parts	to
age	daily	for	low	products	two
all	dairy	from	low-fat	raise	up
also	day	give	made	servings	way
an	diet	goats	main	sheep	what
and	do	good	make	should	why
are	drink	groups	make	slices	will
ask	drinking	grow	milk	so	yogurt
balanced	each	have	much	some	you
better	eat	healthy	muscles	strong	your
body	eating	heart	need	that	
can	farmers	help	of	the	
cheese	fat	how	often	their	
choosing	find	in	one	there	
come	first	is	or	these	

Index

About the Author

Katie Marsico is an author of nonfiction books for children and young adults. She lives outside of Chicago, Illinois, with her husband and children.